Phonetic Storybook 14

all • ar = or • dge • ue, le
x = ks • i̇e = ē • ¢a = ā •
eø = ĕ • ear = er • f to v + es

Raceway Steps 28A–C

MODERN CURRICULUM PRESS
Pearson Learning Group

Contents

The Basketball Team

By Hetty Hubbard

Illustrated by John Magine

Vocabulary Words

basket ball
1. basketball

2. called

3. fall

4. hall

5. small

6. wall

Story Words

bench
7. benches

8. Dobbs

9. grinned

10. hoped

lean
11. leaned

12. Nick

13. Nick's

14. played

15. sure

wait
16. waited

wänt
17. wanted

4

The basketball coach was going to pick the team today. All the kids wanted to be on the team to play in the fall. They waited in the hall to see the coach. Some sat on benches, and some leaned on the wall. The tall kids were sure they would be picked.

The not-so-tall kids
hoped to be on the team,
too. Nick was not-so-tall.
He was small, but he
played basketball very well.
He wished Coach Dobbs
would pick him to be on
the team.

Soon, it was Nick's turn to see the coach.

"Come on in, Nick," the coach called. "I am glad to say you made the team. You may not be tall, but you are fast."

Nick grinned. "Thank you," he said. "I'll do my best for the team!"

The End

No War

By Sue Dickson, Lynda MacDonald,
and J. Lyn Fara

Illustrated by Nathan Young Jarvis

Vocabulary Words

1. re ward
   reward

2. swarm
   swarmed

3. **thwart**

4. **toward**

5. **war**

6. **warm**

7. warn
   warned

8. **Warren**

Story Words

9. ahĕ␀d

10. be came
    became

11. (ch)
    crē␀ture

12. far away
    faraway

13. **flung**

14. (hē rōes)
    heroes

15. hurl
    hurled

16. **landed**

17. **roar**

18. **strānge**

19. **that's**

20. travel
    traveler

21. **travels**

22. E␀rth

9

Warren was a traveler who had no fear.

He came from a planet not far from here.

His travels took him to faraway stars.

He made trips to both Earth and Mars.

One day a bad storm out in space,

Flung his ship all over the place.

Out of space his ship was hurled.

Warren landed on a strange, warm world.

Safe on a beach,
Warren lay down.
   Soon little animals
swarmed all around.
   One animal warned,
"Just hear that roar!
   Hurry, friends, get set
for war!"

A brave one came
toward Warren and said,
"We can thwart a war
if we think ahead.
Tie up this creature with
a long, strong cord.
We will be heroes and
get a reward!"

The animals thought this plan was smart,

But Warren woke up before they could start.

"Let's be friends," he said with a smile.

"I crashed and will be here for awhile."

So, Warren and the animals became friends.

And that is how the story ends!

The End

A Surprise for Mrs. Hodges

By Hetty Hubbard
Illustrated by Martha Avilés

Vocabulary Words

1. bridge
2. budge
3. edge
4. hedge
5. Hodges
6. ledge
7. nudged
8. Park Ridge
9. pledge
10. sledge
11. trudged
12. wedged

Story Words

13. across
14. agreed
15. along
16. broom
17. David
18. every
19. grabbed
20. handle
21. Hodges's
22. light
23. pulled
24. Ramon
25. Ramon's

David and Ramon missed Mrs. Hodges. She is their neighbor. She had been away for two weeks. She had gone to Park Ridge to visit friends.

"Let's fix up her yard," said David.

The boys ran to get some tools. Ramon lifted the latch of the tool shed door to open it.

There was a broom
wedged way in the back.

Ramon lifted some tools
out of the way.

"This sledge hammer is
not light," he said. "It
must weigh a ton!"

At last, Ramon and
David could get to the
broom.

Ramon grabbed the broom. It would not budge! It was caught under the ledge. Ramon held the handle. He nudged it away from the ledge.

David found a bag, a pail, and a weeding tool. "Here we go," he said.

Ramon swept the steps.
Then, he cleaned under
the hedge. David pulled
weeds from the lawn.
The weeds were bad
by the edge of the
driveway.

David and Ramon finished. Then, they trudged back to the shed with their tools. Just then, Mrs. Hodges's car came across the bridge.

"What a nice surprise!" said Mrs. Hodges. "I saw you boys when I came over the bridge. Thank you so much for your help!"

Mrs. Hodges gave the boys a big hug.

It was nice to have a neighbor like Mrs. Hodges. Ramon and David were glad they had fixed up her yard. They made a pledge. They would do her yard every week.

The End

Sue Makes Valentines

By Hetty Hubbard

Illustrated by Bari Weissman

Vocabulary Words

1. clue
2. due
3. flue
4. giggled
5. glue
6. hue
7. little
8. middle
9. Sue
10. true

Story Words

11. carrier
12. dif fer ent
    different
13. Feb ru ary
    February
14. fire light
    firelight
15. fire place
    fireplace
16. guess
17. mail box
    mailbox
18. opened
19. sending
20. sil ver
    silver
21. Sue's
22. used
23. val en tine
    valentine
24. valentines

"February 14 will be here soon," said Sue. "I must finish my valentines."

Sue's mom opened the fireplace flue. The firelight gave the paper a different hue.

"This silver paper sometimes looks blue and sometimes yellow!" said Sue. She giggled.

Sue used glue to add
a little silver paper and
some lace to the middle
of each valentine. Then,
she wrote, "It is true,
I love you." on each one.

Sue did not put her
name on the valentines,
but she gave this clue:
19-21-5. Can you guess?
ABCDEFGHIJKLMN
OPQRSTUVWXYZ

The mail carrier was due to come soon. Sue had to hurry to the mailbox with her valentines.

Sue had fun making and sending pretty valentines to her friends.

The End

Uncle Max

By Hetty Hubbard

Illustrated by Kathleen Kemly

Vocabulary Words

1. ax
2. box
3. fix
4. fox
5. mix
   mixed
6. mixing
7. next
8. ox
9. relax
10. six
11. wax

Story Words

add
12. added

an other
13. another

14. easy

love
15. loved

16. lumpy

nice
17. nicest

18. sharpen

19. Tony

tool box
20. toolbox

Tony loved to help his
Uncle Max. Uncle Max
could fix almost anything.
One time, Tony helped
Uncle Max make a toolbox.
He saw Uncle Max sharpen
an ax. Another time, Tony
helped him clean and wax
his car.

"What will we do next, Uncle Max?" asked Tony.

Uncle Max said, "Could you stir this paint and mix it well for me? It is thick and lumpy."

"Sure," said Tony. He was glad to help. Tony started mixing the paint.

After awhile, Uncle Max
looked to see if the paint
was mixed.

"Well," said Uncle Max,
"I would say you are as
strong as an ox and as
smart as a fox! With such
good help, we can be
finished before six o'clock!"

Tony sat down to relax a bit. Tony thought about Uncle Max. He said the nicest things!

Out loud, Tony said, "Do you really think I am as strong as an ox?"

"Yes, and as smart as a fox!" added Uncle Max.

The End

A Piece of Beanstalk

By Sue Dickson and Lynda MacDonald

Illustrated by Denise Fraifeld

Vocabulary Words

believe
1. believed

2. brief

3. Chief

dis belief
4. disbelief

5. field

6. Greenfield

7. niece

8. piece

9. pier

10. relief

11. shield

12. yield

Story Words

bean stälk
13. beanstalk

14. Denise

every one
15. everyone

every where
16. everywhere

17. giving

18. grew

19. police

20. planted

21. reached

(er)
22. worry

One day, Denise planted a piece of green beanstalk. It was from her niece. Her niece said it would yield a big plant. In a brief time, it began to grow. Denise gave it relief from the sun. She believed in giving it lots of water.

The piece of beanstalk grew and grew. Denise looked at it one day in disbelief! It filled the yard. Then, it filled the whole field! Soon, it filled the town of Greenfield. It reached all the way to the pier by the river. The beanstalk was everywhere!

Everyone in town began to worry. Could they shield the rest of the town from the huge beanstalk? The Chief of Police took action. He said to Denise, "Let's try this. Do not give it any more water."

And that was the end of the beanstalk!

The End

A Bear's Steak

By Sue Dickson and Lynda MacDonald

Illustrated by Eldon Doty

Vocabulary Words

1. bear
2. break
3. great
4. pear
5. steak

Story Words

6. bear's
7. frying
8. woods

At break of day we
saw big Dan,
Pack a steak, a pear,
and a frying pan.

He went to the woods
and started to make,
A fire so he could fix
his steak.

Out of the woods came
a great big bear!
Dan rushed away with
just the pear!

The End

A Breath of Spring

by Sue Dickson and Lynda MacDonald
Illustrated by Jason Wolfe

Vocabulary Words

1. breath
2. dead
3. feather
4. head
5. health
6. Heather
7. Heather's
8. heavy
9. instead
10. read
11. ready
12. steady
13. sweater
14. sweaters
15. thread
16. weather

Story Words

17. fresh
18. later
19. oops
20. perfect
21. pull $(\widecheck{oo})$
22. seagull
23. Skip
24. splinter
25. stretched
26. throw
27. while

"The spring weather is perfect," said Heather. "May we go out in the boat today?" she asked.

"Yes," said Mom. "Put on your sweaters. It is still cool."

"I'm ready," said Skip.

"I'll pull the boat ahead a little. Then, I'll hold it while you get in," said Mom.

"Let me do it instead," said Skip. "The boat is heavy. I will keep it steady while you and Heather get in."

"Oops!" said Skip. "A thread in my sweater is caught on a splinter."

"It will be OK. We can fix it later," said Mom.

"Look at the crab!"
yelled Skip. "I will try to
get it!"

Skip picked up the net
and stretched to get
the crab.

"Oh, it is dead. I will
throw it back in," he said.

Heather took a deep breath. "I love spring," she said.

Just then a seagull flew over the boat. A feather floated down onto Heather's head. "Look! A feather!" she yelled.

"Look!" cried Skip. "They are getting a fish!"

"I read that eating fish is good for your health," said Heather.

"Yes, and we may have fish for dinner," Mom said. "We can have fresh bread and butter, too!"

The End

The Search for the Pearls

By Rick Pantale, Sue Dickson, and
Lynda MacDonald

Illustrated by Diane Palmisciano

Vocabulary Words

1. Earl
2. early
3. earned
4. heard
5. knife
6. learned
   life
7. lives
   loaf
8. loaves
9. Pearls
10. Search
11. searched
    thief
12. Thieves'
    wife
13. wives

Story Words

14. brothers
15. chests
16. dōve
17. Grandfather
18. Grandmother
19. hauled
20. Island
21. jewels
22. museum
23. pirate
24. raking
25. should
26. someday
27. sunk

"Have you ever heard
the story 'The Search for
the Pearls'?" asked
Grandfather.

Earl said, "No, I never
heard that one."

"When we finish raking
these leaves, I will tell
you," said Grandfather.

Grandmother called from
the porch. "I just baked
three loaves of bread.
Come in and I will cut a
fresh slice for you. You
have earned it," she said.

Grandfather and Earl ran into the house. Grandmother had a sharp knife. She cut some slices from one loaf for them.

"This is good bread, dear," said Grandfather.

"Thank you," said Grandmother.

When they finished eating, Grandfather began his story.

"Once upon a time, there were two brothers, Sam and Ben. All their lives they wanted to search for pearls. So, one day they did. Their wives, Nell and Liz, went with them."

"They learned that a pirate ship had sunk in the sea off Thieves' Island. On the ship there was a huge chest of fine pearls."

"Early one morning, Sam and Ben and their wives set out to search for the pearls."

"They searched and searched for days and days. At last, they found the chest!"

Grandfather went on: "They hauled up the chest of pearls from the sea!"

"Then, Sam and Ben and their wives dove back down to search for more pearls. What do you think they found?"

"More pearls?" asked Earl.

"No," said Grandfather. "They found a chest of jewels. They hauled it up out of the sea. They gave both chests to a museum because there were so many gems."

"Why did they give the chests to a museum?" asked Earl.

"So that everyone could enjoy the pearls and jewels they found!"

"Wow!" said Earl. "Maybe I should go search for pearls and jewels!"

"Maybe you will do that someday!" said Grandfather with a smile.

The End